LET'S INVESTIGATE

Trucks

JOHN HUDSON TINER

Published by Creative Paperbacks
123 South Broad Street, Mankato, Minnesota 56001
Creative Paperbacks is an imprint of The Creative Company

Art direction by Rita Marshall
Production design by The Design Lab

Photographs by Corbis (David Keaton, Charles O'Rear, Galen Rowell), Gregory A. Fischer,
Richard Gross, Wernher Krutein (photovault.com), Sally McCrae Kuyper, Mack Trucks, Inc.,
Bonnie Sue Rauch, Drew Ryder, D. Jeanene Tiner, Unicorn Stock Photos (B.W. Hoffmann)

Library of Congress Cataloging-in-Publication Data

The Library of Congress has cataloged the hardcover edition as follows:
Tiner, John Hudson, 1944–
Trucks / by John Hudson Tiner.
p. cm. — (Let's investigate)
Summary: An introduction to the history of trucks and to
various kinds of trucks of the past, present, and future.
ISBN 0-89812-392-5 (paperback)
ISBN 1-58341-259-X (hardcover)
1. Trucks—Juvenile literature. [1. Trucks.] I. Title. II. Series.
TL230.15 .T56   2003
629.224—dc21   2002035133

First Paperback Edition

2 4 6 8 9 7 5 3 1

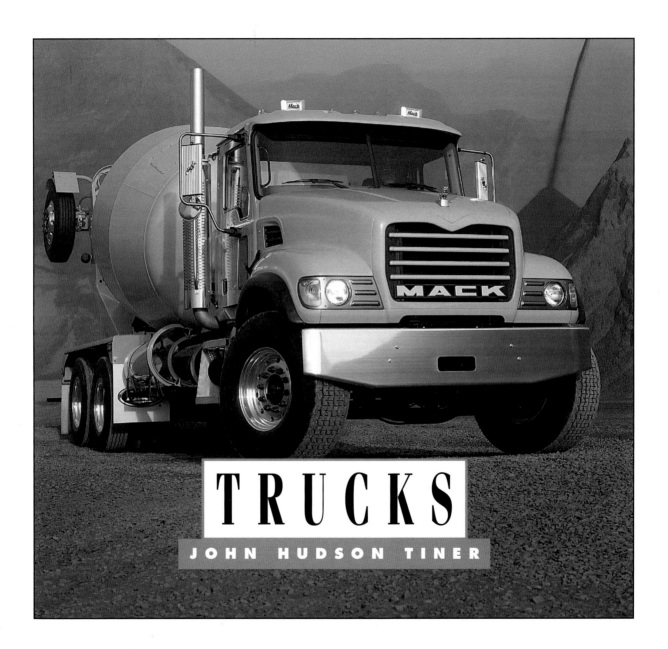

TRUCKS

JOHN HUDSON TINER

CREATIVE
PAPER BACKS

TRUCK
NUMBERS

There are about two million semis in the United States and Canada. They are far outnumbered by pickup trucks and sport utility vehicles, which number about 75 million.

4

TRUCK
HAULING

Moving vans are used to transport furnishings when people move to a new home. The goods are often packed in padded boxes and tied down so they do not shake around.

Trucks are used to haul a wide array of cargo, from dirt to appliances

Trucks are vehicles used mainly to haul **cargo** from one place to another. Some are barely bigger than a car, while others are large enough to haul a whole collection of cars. Almost everything found in a person's home, such as food, furniture, and **appliances**, was brought at least part of the way by a truck. By hauling cargo, and in some cases by carrying people, trucks make our lives easier in a number of ways.

*Laws limit the
lengths of tractor-
trailers. Some trac-
tor cabs are built
over the engine so
the trailer can be
longer. The cab tilts
up when mechanics
need to work on
the engine.*

6

*Many tractors have a
long nose to house the
truck's powerful engine*

BIG TRUCKS

The largest trucks are called tractor-trailers and are divided into two parts. The front part is the tractor, which has the engine and the **cab**. The other part is a trailer that is attached to the tractor. Tractor-trailers are also called "semis" because the trailer is actually a semi-trailer—it has one set of wheels at the back but none at the front, which rests on the tractor.

7

A tractor-trailer truck is about 80 feet (24 m) long from the front bumper to the doors at the rear of the trailer. It is about 13 1/2 feet (4.1 m) high and 8 1/2 feet (2.6 m) wide. A tractor-trailer has a powerful 500-**horsepower** engine that allows it to move heavy cargo. When fully loaded, a tractor-trailer can weigh as much as 80,000 pounds (36,360 kg).

Tractor-trailers share the road with cars and motorcycles

TRUCK
WARNING

When a flatbed trailer carries an oversized load, a smaller vehicle with flashing lights, known as an escort vehicle, goes in front to warn drivers that a wide load is coming.

There are three main types of trailers: enclosed containers, flatbeds, and tanks. An enclosed trailer hauls food, paper, appliances, and other goods. The trailer's sides and top keep the goods from being damaged by rain and reduces the chances of them being stolen. An enclosed refrigerated trailer is used to haul cargo that must be kept cool or frozen, such as meat, fish, or ice cream. The refrigerator pumps cold air into the trailer so the food will not spoil.

Flatbed trailers have no sides or top. They are used to carry loads such as pipes, logs, or cargo of an odd size. Strong chains or cables hold the cargo in place. Flatbed trailers are

also used to move bulldozers and other construction equipment. Flatbed trailers can carry loads that stick out on each side. A truck pulling an oversized load has flashing lights and red flags that warn other drivers that it is coming. Banners reading "Wide Load" are attached to the front and back of the truck.

TRUCK
HEIGHT

Some flatbed trailers are made low to the roadway so they can carry tall equipment and still fit under overpass bridges. This kind of flatbed trailer is called a "low boy."

TRUCK
CARGO

Some tractor-trailers pull flatbeds with cargo in large aluminum containers. The containers can be lifted off the trailer and put on railroad flatcars or hoisted aboard a ship.

Flatbed trailers can handle all kinds of large, irregular-shaped loads

TRUCK
TANKS

A tractor-trailer has two fuel tanks that together hold about 240 gallons (872 l) of fuel. A tractor-trailer can go about 1,500 miles (2,400 km) without refueling.

TRUCK
FEES

Trucks that haul cargo between states pay road fees in each state. In addition, government taxes are collected on the fuel that is used to power the trucks' engines.

Attached to two tanker trailers, this semi is pulling a heavy load

Tankers are trailers that haul liquids. These liquids might be foods such as milk or syrup, or they may be chemicals such as acids or compressed gas. When a truck hauls dangerous chemicals, a sign is placed on the tank describing what is inside. That way, if the truck is in an accident, firefighters know what kind of fluids might be leaking out.

11

T railers come in other forms, too. Some, called piggyback trailers, are hauled on train flatcars. The entire trailer, including the wheels, is put on a flatcar and held in place with chains. A car carrier is a special-purpose trailer that has ramps to load and transport cars, including a ramp that extends over the truck's cab. The cars are chained in place so they do not roll off. A car carrier can haul nine or more regular size cars at once.

Aboard a trailer, a car can move long distances with a minimum of wear

TRUCK
NICKNAMES

Tractor-trailers are known as "18-wheelers" because they have a total of 18 wheels. They are also called "big rigs."

12

TRUCK
PAY

Truck drivers are paid by the number of miles that they drive. Trucking companies charge their customers by the weight of the freight that is hauled, as well as the distance.

A semi's sleeper compartment is a trucker's home away from home

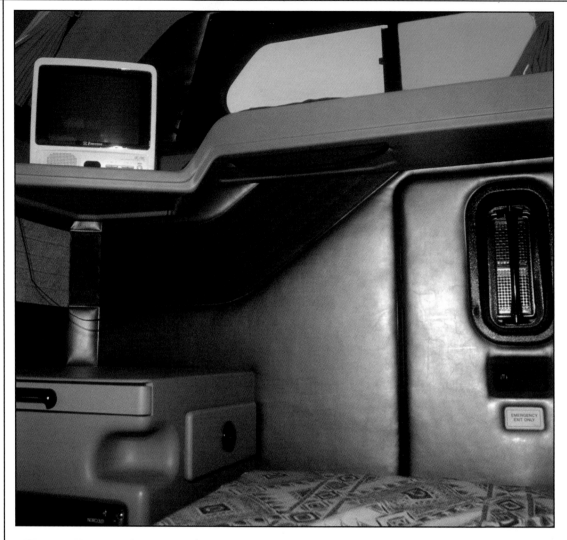

ost tractor-trailers haul cargo between cities. Drivers often have to spend the night away from home. Behind the driver's seat in the cab of many trucks is a sleeper compartment with a bed for the driver and storage space for clothes. A driver might also put a small television, microwave oven, or refrigerator in the cab.

TRUCKS AROUND TOWN

Because tractor-trailers are so long, they are seldom used to make deliveries inside big cities. Instead, the goods are taken off tractor-trailers, stored in **warehouses**, and then loaded onto smaller trucks called delivery trucks.

TRUCK
MILEAGE

Most tractor-trailers burn about a gallon (3.8 l) of fuel for every six to eight miles (10–13 km) that they travel.

TRUCK
DELIVERY

Tanker trucks may be used to deliver gasoline to underground fuel tanks at gas stations. A tanker truck can carry about 6,500 gallons (24,600 l) of fuel.

Delivery trucks are big and powerful, yet get around easily on city streets

TRUCK GROUP

*Most truck drivers in the U.S. belong to a **trade union** known as the Teamsters. The name comes from the way trailers were first pulled—by teams of horses.*

Trucks that are smaller than tractor-trailers are built as a single unit. A frame connects the engine, cab, and bed (area where the cargo is carried). Most delivery trucks are enclosed, and the back part is called the box. Most boxes are 15 to 27 feet (4.6–8.2 m) long, 8 feet (2.4 m) wide, and 8 feet (2.4 m) high. Some delivery trucks, such as those that carry soft drinks, are built with doors along the side so the driver can easily reach the product he or she is hauling.

TRUCK
LICENSE

Most states require drivers to have a special driver's license, called a commercial license, to drive trucks that are used for business.

TRUCK
TALK

Truckers communicate with one another by citizens band (CB) radio. They exchange information about road conditions, traffic jams, and weather forecasts.

D elivery trucks carry a variety of goods. They haul furniture from stores to homes. They bring bread, soft drinks, cookies, and other groceries to supermarkets and restaurants. On some delivery trucks, a lift in back folds downs and acts as a moveable platform to lower heavy items to the ground.

Far left, a parcel delivery truck Left, a side-opening soft drink truck

TRUCK
CARE

Garbage trucks collect trash and household refuse. Some garbage trucks are loaded by workers who ride on the back of the truck. When the truck stops, they jump off and empty garbage cans into the back of the truck. Other trucks have a metal arm that fits into a garbage bin. The driver positions his or her truck just right and pulls a lever to raise the garbage bin and tilt it upside down to empty the garbage into the truck.

A garbage truck

TRUCK VALUE

Each truck tire on a semi costs about $500, so the total value of the 18 tires and two spare tires on a tractor-trailer is about $10,000.

EMERGENCY TRUCKS

Many trucks are made for use in emergencies. A pumper is a fire truck with a tank that holds about 500 gallons (1,900 l) of water. It has a powerful pump for spraying water through a long hose onto fires. The pump can empty the tank in less than a minute. Before the tank runs out, firefighters attach hoses to a **hydrant** or drop a hose in a nearby source of water such as a lake, river, or swimming pool and use that water to fight the fire. Like all emergency vehicles, a pumper has flashing lights to warn other drivers that it is coming.

Equipped with a wailing siren and flashing lights, a pumper moves quickly

TRUCK
REACH

A cherry picker is a truck with a platform that allows workers to repair high wires. It is called a cherry picker because the platform goes high enough to reach the top of a cherry tree.

TRUCK
DIFFERENCE

Vehicles in the U.S. have the steering wheel and other driver controls on the left side. In England, Scotland, and Australia, these controls are on the vehicle's right side.

Firefighters climbing the extended ladder of a ladder truck

Another type of fire truck, called a ladder truck, carries a ladder that can extend about 100 feet (30 m) into the air. Firefighters with a hose climb the ladder to direct water onto the flames. Firefighters can also use the ladder to rescue people who are trapped on the upper floors of a burning building.

Rescue trucks usually travel with firefighters to provide emergency medical service. Rescue trucks, more commonly called ambulances, are equipped to treat injured or sick people and to transport them quickly to a hospital. An ambulance carries emergency medical personnel who can give injured people **blood transfusions**, provide oxygen to those having difficulty breathing, give people painkillers, and treat burns and cuts.

The first ambulances were pulled by horses. The first motorized ambulances were used during World War I (1914–1918).

19

Ambulances have wide-opening rear doors

TRUCK
TOWING

Tow trucks are also called "wreckers" because they often haul vehicles that have been wrecked in traffic accidents.

Tow trucks improve traffic by hauling wrecked or stalled vehicles from roads

A tow truck is an emergency vehicle designed to move cars or trucks that need repair, such as those damaged by a traffic accident. Some have tilt-down beds and **winches** that pull the disabled car up on the bed. Others haul the car by putting a lift under the car's front wheels. Tow trucks also have a metal hook at the end of a steel cable to pull stuck vehicles out of mud or snow. Once the hook is attached to the vehicle, a motor on the truck turns a winch that winds in the cable and pulls the vehicle onto the road.

TRUCK

Some trucks used inside large ware- houses are powered by electric motors that get their elec- tricity from recharge- able batteries.

21

TRUCK
TRANSPORT

*More people ride buses each day than they do any other form of **public transportation**, including airplanes, trains, and taxis.*

TRUCKS FOR PEOPLE

A bus is a type of truck designed to carry a lot of people. Tour buses are buses that usually carry people on vacations. They have comfortable seats, large windows, enough space for luggage on long trips, and a restroom built in the back. City buses carry people on short trips, so there is no room for luggage. A city bus holds about 50 seated passengers, but more can crowd on board by standing and holding on to overhead rails. In England, buses have double decks so they can carry more people. School buses carry children. They are painted yellow and have foldout stop signs so traffic will stop when children are boarding or getting off.

Many children ride a school bus every day

Drivers of recreational vehicles (RVs) may park in campgrounds with hookups to water and electricity. Most parks have a dump station where an RV's restroom holding tank can be emptied.

23

S ome trucks are used as homes away from home. Recreational vehicles (RVs) are trucks that people drive while on vacation. A motor home is a type of RV that includes many of the same comforts found at home. Some motor homes are 40 feet (12 m) long and have a kitchen, bathroom, and one or more bedrooms.

Motor homes are a luxurious way to travel and see the countryside

TRUCK

CLASSES

A pickup truck is classified as a light truck: it can carry no more than 5,000 pounds (2,270 kg). A tractor-trailer is a heavy truck: it can carry more than 33,000 pounds (15,000 kg).

Even small pickups can handle rugged terrain much better than a car can

Pickup trucks are the smallest type of truck. Most have only one bench seat with room for a driver and one or two passengers. Pickups have small beds that can hold light loads such as lawn mowers or furniture. Pickups are popular with farmers, carpenters, outdoorsmen, and other people who frequently haul tools or equipment or drive over rugged land.

TRUCK
SERVICE

The first motorized buses began regular service in Germany in 1895. Today, the Greyhound Company runs the main passenger bus line between U.S. cities.

TRUCK

PLOW

A snow removal truck, also called a snowplow, has a blade in front for pushing snow off of roadways.

*Above, a snowplow
Right, SUVs have
become very popular
in the U.S.*

A sport utility vehicle (SUV) is a type of small truck used mainly to carry passengers. Many SUVs have four-wheel drive, which means that power from the engine turns all four wheels (instead of two as in most vehicles). With all four wheels turning, a SUV can go through snow and mud better than a passenger car. Some people like to drive SUVs because the vehicles sit higher off the ground, and drivers can see the road better.

Some trucks are designed for unique tasks. An armored truck has steel walls and bullet-proof windows and is used to transport money. A paddy wagon is a type of police truck built to carry prisoners. Electricity and telephone companies use trucks that have a long metal arm with a platform attached to the end. The arm can unfold and stretch into the air to lift workers high enough to repair wires on tall poles.

TRUCK
PLATES

Both SUVs and pick-ups are considered small trucks by the U.S. government. However, most states give them license plates as if they were passenger cars.

27

This truck easily puts workers in a position to repair telephone wires

28

A **concrete** truck has a large tank on the back that is constantly turning around and around. The tank, or drum, carries a mixture of water, sand, gravel, and a type of powdered stone called cement. When the mixture is allowed to harden, it forms concrete. Concrete is used at building sites to make foundations, walls, and sidewalks. The rotating tank of a concrete truck keeps the concrete well mixed. If the tank stopped turning, the mixture inside would get hard before it was delivered to the building site. Concrete trucks carry a trough or pipe to pour the mixture out at the site.

Concrete trucks and their rotating drums are common at construction sites

*Most small trucks
are powered by gaso-
line, the type of fuel
used in cars. Larger
trucks use diesel
fuel, which is similar
to gasoline but is
less expensive.*

29

A dump truck has an open bin on the back used to carry loose material such as dirt, sand, or broken rock. When building a road or digging a foundation for a building, construction workers often need to move dirt and rock from one place to another. Once the material reaches its final destination, the bin raises to dump the truck's load.

*A single dump truck can
move many tons of dirt
and rock in a single day*

TRUCK
REVERSAL

The U.S. Postal Service has trucks with the steering wheels and driver controls on the right side so it is easier for drivers to put mail in curbside mailboxes.

Whether carrying wood, food, or passengers, trucks are a big part of our lives

Trucks are one of the most widely used means of transporting goods in the world today. Tractor-trailer trucks haul cargo between cities before handing the goods off to delivery trucks, which move throughout cities to bring the goods to stores or homes. And from buses to RVs to SUVs, trucks play a big role in getting people around, too.

Glossary

Appliances are electrical devices such as refrigerators and dishwashers.

Blood transfusions are transfers of blood from a healthy person to a sick or injured person.

A **cab** is the front part of a truck where the driver sits and operates the vehicle.

The material that a truck carries is called **cargo**; it may also be called "freight" or "load."

Concrete is a substance that can be poured when wet but becomes as hard as stone when it dries.

Horsepower is a measurement of the speed at which an engine does work. A 1.0 horsepower engine can lift 55 pounds (25 kg) to a height of 10 feet (3 m) in one second.

A fire **hydrant** is an upright pipe connected to an underground water line; fire hoses can be connected to it.

License plates are metal plates attached to vehicles; they have numbers and letters that identify the vehicle.

A truck driver writes official information about the operation of the truck in a **logbook**.

Public transportation is a system that helps people travel for a fee; taxis and city buses are part of the system.

People who work at the same type of job may join an organization called a **trade union** that tries to improve their wages and working conditions.

Warehouses are temporary storage buildings for cargo.

Winches are motor-driven, cylinder-shaped drums that turn to wind in a cable that's attached to a load that needs to be moved.

Index